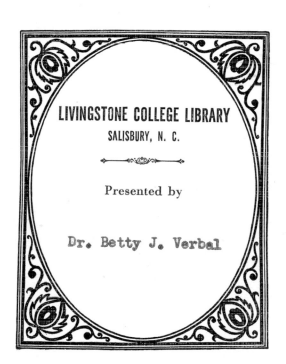

Education

By IMMANUEL KANT

ANN ARBOR PAPERBACKS

The University of Michigan Press

FIRST EDITION AS AN ANN ARBOR PAPERBACK 1960
ALL RIGHTS RESERVED
SECOND PRINTING 1964
PUBLISHED IN THE UNITED STATES OF AMERICA BY
THE UNIVERSITY OF MICHIGAN PRESS AND SIMULTANEOUSLY
IN TORONTO, CANADA, BY AMBASSADOR BOOKS LIMITED
TRANSLATED BY ANNETTE CHURTON
MANUFACTURED IN THE UNITED STATES OF AMERICA

CONTENTS

—◦◇◦—

EDUCATION

CHAPTER I

INTRODUCTION

1. MAN is the only being who needs education. For by education we must understand nurture (the tending and feeding of the child), discipline (*Zucht*), and teaching, together with culture.[1] According to this, man is in succession infant (requiring nursing), child (requiring discipline), and scholar (requiring teaching).

2. Animals use their powers, as soon as they are possessed of them, according to a regular plan—that is, in a way not harmful to themselves.

---

[1] Culture (*Bildung*) is used here in the sense of moral training.—(Tr.)

It is indeed wonderful, for instance, that young swallows, when newly hatched and still blind, are careful not to defile their nests.

Animals therefore need no nurture, but at the most, food, warmth, and guidance, or a kind of protection. It is true, most animals need feeding, but they do not require nurture. For by nurture we mean the tender care and attention which parents must bestow upon their children, so as to prevent them from using their powers in a way which would be harmful to themselves. For instance, should an animal cry when it comes into the world, as children do, it would surely become a prey to wolves and other wild animals, which would gather round, attracted by its cry.

3. Discipline changes animal nature into human nature. Animals are by their instinct all that they ever can be; some other reason has provided everything for them at the outset. But man needs a reason of his own. Having no instinct, he has to work out a plan of conduct for himself. Since, however, he is not able to do this all at once, but comes into the world undeveloped, others have to do it for him.

4. All the natural endowments of mankind

must be developed little by little out of man himself, through his own effort.

One generation educates the next. The first beginnings of this process of educating may be looked for either in a rude and unformed, or in a fully developed condition of man. If we assume the latter to have come first, man must at all events afterwards have degenerated and lapsed into barbarism.

It is discipline, which prevents man from being turned aside by his animal impulses from humanity, his appointed end. Discipline, for instance, must restrain him from venturing wildly and rashly into danger. Discipline, thus, is merely negative, its action being to counteract man's natural unruliness. The positive part of education is instruction.

Unruliness consists in independence of law. By discipline men are placed in subjection to the laws of mankind, and brought to feel their constraint. This, however, must be accomplished early. Children, for instance, are first sent to school, not so much with the object of their learning something, but rather that they may become used to sitting still and doing exactly as they are told. And this to the end that in later life they should not wish to put actually and instantly into practice anything that strikes them.

5. The love of freedom is naturally so strong in man, that when once he has grown accustomed to freedom, he will sacrifice everything for its sake. For this very reason discipline must be brought into play very early; for when this has not been done, it is difficult to alter character later in life. Undisciplined men are apt to follow every caprice.

We see this also among savage nations, who, though they may discharge functions for some time like Europeans, yet can never become accustomed to European manners. With them, however, it is not the noble love of freedom which Rousseau and others imagine, but a kind of barbarism—the animal, so to speak, not having yet developed its human nature. Men should therefore accustom themselves early to yield to the commands of reason, for if a man be allowed to follow his own will in his youth, without opposition, a certain lawlessness will cling to him throughout his life. And it is no advantage to such a man that in his youth he has been spared through an over-abundance of

motherly tenderness, for later on all the more
will he have to face opposition from all sides,
and constantly receive rebuffs, as soon as he
enters into the business of the world.

It is a common mistake made in the education of those of high rank, that because they are
hereafter to become rulers they must on that
account receive no opposition in their youth.
Owing to his natural love of freedom it is
necessary that man should have his natural
roughness smoothed down ; with animals, their
instinct renders this unnecessary.

6. Man needs nurture and culture. Culture
includes discipline and *instruction*. These, as
far as we know, no animal needs, for none of
them learn anything from their elders, except
birds, who are taught by them to sing; and it is
a touching sight to watch the mother bird
singing with all her might to her young ones,
who, like children at school, stand round and try
to produce the same tones out of their tiny
throats. In order to convince ourselves that
birds do not sing by instinct, but that they are
actually taught to sing, it is worth while to make
an experiment. Suppose we take away half the
eggs from a canary, and put sparrow's eggs in

their place, or exchange young sparrows for young canaries; if the young birds are then brought into a room where they cannot hear the sparrows outside, they will learn the canary's song, and we thus get singing sparrows. It is, indeed, very wonderful that each species of bird has its own peculiar song, which is preserved unchanged through all its generations; and the tradition of the song is probably the most faithful in the world.

7. Man can only become man by education. He is merely what education makes of him. It is noticeable that man is only educated by man —that is, by men who have themselves been educated. Hence with some people it is want of discipline and instruction on their own part, which makes them in turn unfit educators of their pupils. Were some being of higher nature than man to undertake our education, we should then be able to see what man might become. It is, however, difficult for us accurately to estimate man's natural capabilities, since some things are imparted to man by education, while other things are only developed by education. Were it possible, by the help of those in high rank, and through the united forces of many people, to

make an experiment on this question, we might even by this means be able to gain some information as to the degree of eminence which it is possible for man to attain. But it is as important to the speculative mind, as it is sad to one who loves his fellow-men, to see how those in high rank generally care only for their own concerns, and take no part in the important experiments of education, which bring our nature one step nearer to perfection.

There is no one who, having been neglected in his youth, can come to years of discretion without knowing whether the defect lies in discipline or culture (for so we may call instruction). The uncultivated man is crude, the undisciplined is unruly. Neglect of discipline is a greater evil than neglect of culture, for this last can be remedied later in life, but unruliness cannot be done away with, and a mistake in discipline can never be repaired. It may be that education will be constantly improved, and that each succeeding generation will advance one step towards the perfecting of mankind; for with education is involved the great secret of the perfection of human nature. It is only now that something may be done in this direction, since for the first time people have begun to judge rightly, and understand clearly, what actually belongs to a good education. It is delightful to realise that through education human nature will be continually improved, and brought to such a condition as is worthy of the nature of man. This opens out to us the prospect of a happier human race in the future.

8. The prospect of a *theory of education* is a glorious ideal, and it matters little if we are not able to realise it at once. Only we must not look upon the idea as chimerical, nor decry it as a beautiful dream, notwithstanding the difficulties that stand in the way of its realisation.

An idea is nothing else than the conception of a perfection which has not yet been experienced. For instance, the idea of a perfect republic governed by principles of justice—is such an idea impossible, because it has not yet been experienced?

Our idea must in the first place be correct, and then, notwithstanding all the hindrances that still stand in the way of its realisation, it is not at all impossible. Suppose, for instance, lying to become universal, would truth-speaking on that account become nothing but a whim?

And the idea of an education which will develop all man's natural gifts is certainly a true one.

9. Under the present educational system man does not fully attain to the object of his being; for in what various ways men live! Uniformity can only result when all men act according to the same principles, which principles would have to become with them a second nature. What we can do is to work out a scheme of education better suited to further its objects, and hand down to posterity directions as to how this scheme may be carried into practice, so that they might be able to realise it gradually. Take the auricula as an example. When raised from a root this plant bears flowers of one colour only; when raised from seed, the flowers are of the most varied colours. Nature has placed these manifold germs in the plant, and their development is only a question of proper sowing and planting. Thus it is with man.

10. There are many germs lying undeveloped in man. It is for us to make these germs grow, by *developing his natural gifts* in their due proportion, and to see that he fulfils his destiny. Animals accomplish this for them-

selves unconsciously. Man must strive to
attain it, but this he cannot do if he has not
even a conception as to the object of his
existence. For the individual it is absolutely
impossible to attain this object. Let us suppose
the first parents to have been fully developed, and
see how they educate their children. These
first parents set their children an example, which
the children imitate and in this way develop
some of their own natural gifts. All their gifts
cannot, however, be developed in this way, for
it all depends on occasional circumstances what
examples children see. In times past men had
no conception of the perfection to which human
nature might attain—even now we have not a
very clear idea of the matter. This much,
however, is certain : that no individual man, no
matter what degree of culture may be reached
by his pupils, can insure their attaining their
destiny. To succeed in this, not the work of a
few individuals only is necessary, but that of
the whole human race.

11. Education is an *art* which can only
become perfect through the practice of many
generations. Each generation, provided with
the knowledge of the foregoing one, is able more

and more to bring about an education which shall develop man's natural gifts in their due proportion and in relation to their end, and thus advance the whole human race towards its destiny. Providence has willed, that man shall bring forth for himself the good that lies hidden in his nature, and has spoken, as it were, thus to man : 'Go forth into the world! I have equipped thee with every tendency towards the good. Thy part let it be to develop those tendencies. Thy happiness and unhappiness depend upon thyself alone.'

12. Man must develop his tendency towards *the good.* Providence has not placed goodness ready formed in him, but merely as a tendency and without the distinction of moral law. Man's duty is to improve himself ; to cultivate his mind ; and, when he finds himself going astray, to bring the moral law to bear upon himself. Upon reflection we shall find this very difficult. Hence the greatest and most difficult problem to which man can devote himself is the problem of education. For insight depends on education, and education in its turn depends on insight. It follows therefore that education can only advance by

slow degrees, and a true conception of the method of education can only arise when one generation transmits to the next its stores of experience and knowledge, each generation adding something of its own before transmitting them to the following. What vast culture and experience does not this conception presuppose? It could only be arrived at at a late stage, and we ourselves have not fully realised this conception. The question arises, Should we in the education of the individual imitate the course followed by the education of the human race through its successive generations?

There are two human inventions which may be considered more difficult than any others— the art of government, and the art of education; and people still contend as to their very meaning.

13. But in developing human talents *where are we to take our stand?* Shall we begin with a rude, or with an already developed state of society?

It is difficult to conceive a development from a state of rudeness (hence it is so difficult to understand what the first man was like), and we see that in a development out of such a condition man has invariably fallen back again into that condition, and has raised himself out of it. In the earliest records of even very civilised nations we still find a distinct taint of barbarism, and yet how much culture is presupposed for mere writing to be possible! So much so that, with regard to civilised people, the beginning of the art of writing might be called the beginning of the world.

14. Since the development of man's natural gifts does not take place of itself, all education is an art. Nature has placed no instinct in him for that purpose. The *origin* as well as the *carrying out* of this art is either *mechanical* and without plan, ruled by given circumstances, or it involves the exercise of *judgment*. The art of education is only then mechanical, when on chance occasions we learn by experience whether anything is useful or harmful to man. All education which is merely mechanical must carry with it many mistakes and deficiencies, because it has no sure principle to work upon. If education is to develop human nature so that it may attain the object of its being, it must involve the exercise of judgment. Educated parents are examples which children use for their

guidance. If, however, the children are to progress beyond their parents, education must become a study, otherwise we can hope for nothing from it, and one man whose education has been spoilt will only repeat his own mistakes in trying to educate others. The mechanism of education must be changed into a science,[1] and one generation may have to pull down what another had built up.

15. One *principle of education* which those men especially who form educational schemes should keep before their eyes is this—children ought to be educated, not for the present, but for a possibly improved condition of man in the future; that is, in a manner which is adapted to the *idea of humanity* and the whole destiny of man. This principle is of great importance. Parents usually educate their children merely in such a manner that, however bad the world may be, they may adapt themselves to its present conditions. But they ought to give them an education so much better than this, that a better condition of things may thereby be brought about in the future.

---

[1] Rink and Schubert add here: ' otherwise it will never be a consistent pursuit.'—(Tr.)

16. Here, however, we are met by two difficulties—(*a*) parents usually only care that their children *make their way* in the world, and (*b*) Sovereigns look upon their subjects merely as *tools* for their own purposes.

Parents care for the home, rulers for the state. Neither have as their aim the universal good and the perfection to which man is destined, and for which he has also a natural disposition. But the basis of a scheme of education must be cosmopolitan. And is, then, the idea of the universal good harmful to us as individuals? Never! for though it may appear that something must be sacrificed by this idea, an advance is also made towards what is the best even for the individual under his present conditions. And then what glorious consequences follow! It is through good education that all the good in the world arises. For this the germs which lie hidden in man need only to be more and more developed; for the rudiments of evil are not to be found in the natural disposition of man. Evil is only the result of nature not being brought under control. In man there are only germs of good.

17. But by whom is the better condition of

the world to be brought about? By rulers or by their subjects? Is it by the latter, who shall so improve themselves that they meet half-way the measures for their good which the government might establish? Were it to depend upon rulers, their own education will first have to be improved, for this has for a long time suffered, owing to the great mistake that they have been allowed to meet with no opposition in their youth.

A tree which stands in a field alone grows crooked and spreads wide its branches; while a tree which stands in the middle of a forest, with the pressure of other trees around, grows tall and straight, seeking air and sunshine from above. It is the same with rulers. In any case it is always better that they should be educated by some one among their subjects, rather than by one of themselves. We can therefore only expect progress to be brought about by rulers if their education has been of a higher kind than that of their subjects.

It depends, then, mainly upon private effort, and not so much on the help of rulers, as Basedow and others supposed; for we find by experience that they have not the universal

good so much in view, as the well-being of the
state, whereby they may attain their own ends.
If, however, they provide funds for this object,
the drawing up of the scheme must be deferred
to them. So it is with everything which concerns the perfection of man's intellect and the
widening of his knowledge. Influence and money
alone cannot do it; they can only lighten the
task. They might do it, if only the financial
authorities of the state were not so anxious to
calculate beforehand the interests which any
sums spent for this purpose might bear for the
treasury. Even academic bodies hitherto have
not undertaken the task, and the likelihood that
they will do so in the future is now as small as
over.

The management of schools ought, then, to
depend entirely upon the judgment of the most
enlightened experts. All culture begins with
the individual, one man gradually influencing
others. It is only through the efforts of people
of broader views, who take an interest in the
universal good, and who are capable of enter-
taining the idea of a better condition of things
in the future, that the gradual progress of
human nature towards its goal is possible. Do

we not still meet, now and then, with a ruler
who looks upon his people merely as forming
part of the animal kingdom, and whose aim it
is merely to propagate the human species?   If
he considers the subject of training the intellect
at all, it is merely in order that his people may
be of more use to him in working out his own
ends. It is, of course, necessary for private
individuals to keep this natural end in view,
but they must also bear in mind more particularly the development of mankind, and see to it
that men become not only clever, but good; and,
what is most difficult, they must seek to bring
posterity nearer to a state of perfection than they
have themselves attained.

18. Through education, then, man must be
made—

First, subject to *discipline*; by which we
must understand that influence which is always
restraining our animal nature from getting the
better of our manhood, either in the individual
as such, or in man as a member of society.
Discipline, then, is merely restraining unruliness.

Secondly, education must also supply men
with *culture*. This includes information and

instruction. It is culture which brings out ability. Ability is the possession of a faculty which is capable of being adapted to various ends. Ability, therefore, does not determine any ends, but leaves that to circumstances as they arise afterwards.

Some accomplishments are essentially good for everybody—reading and writing, for instance; others, merely in the pursuit of certain objects, such as music, which we pursue in order to make ourselves liked. Indeed, the various purposes to which ability may be put are almost endless.

Thirdly, education must also supply a person with *discretion* (*Klugheit*), so that he may be able to conduct himself in society, that he may be liked, and that he may gain influence. For this a kind of culture is necessary which we call *refinement* (*Civilisierung*). The latter requires manners, courtesy, and a kind of discretion which will enable him to use all men for his own ends. This refinement changes according to the ever-changing tastes of different ages. Thus some twenty or thirty years ago ceremonies in social intercourse were still the fashion.

Fourthly, *moral training* must form a part of education. It is not enough that a man shall be fitted for any end, but his disposition must be so trained that he shall choose none but good ends—good ends being those which are necessarily approved by everyone, and which may at the same time be the aim of everyone.

19. Man may be either broken in, trained, and mechanically taught, or he may be really enlightened. Horses and dogs are broken in; and man, too, may be broken in.

It is, however, not enough that children should be merely broken in; for it is of greater importance that they shall learn to *think*. By learning to think, man comes to act according to fixed principles and not at random. Thus we see that a real education implies a great deal. But as a rule, in our private education *the fourth and most important point is still too much neglected*, children being for the most part educated in such a way that moral training is left to the Church. And yet how important it is that children should learn from their youth up to detest vice;—not merely on the ground that God has forbidden it, but because vice is detestable in itself. If children do not learn this early, they are very likely to think that, if only God had not forbidden it, there would be no harm in practising wickedness, and that it would otherwise be allowed, and that therefore He would probably make an exception now and then. But God is the most holy being, and wills only what is good, and desires that we may love virtue for its own sake, and not merely because He requires it.

We live in an age of discipline, culture, and refinement, but we are still a long way off from the age of moral training. According to the present conditions of mankind, one might say that the prosperity of the state grows side by side with the misery of the people. Indeed, it is still a question whether we should not be happier in an uncivilised condition, where all the culture of the present time would find no place, than we are in the present state of society; for how can man be made happy, unless he is first made wise and good? And until this is made our first aim the amount of evil will not be lessened.

20. *Experimental schools* must first be established before we can establish *normal schools*.

Education and instruction must not be merely mechanical; they must be founded upon fixed principles; although at the same time education must not merely proceed by way of reasoning, but must be, in a certain sense, mechanical.

In Austria the greater number of schools used to be normal schools, and these were founded and carried on after a fixed plan, against which much has been said, not without reason. The chief complaint against them was this, that the teaching in them was merely mechanical. But all other schools were obliged to form themselves after the pattern of these normal schools, because government even refused to promote persons who had not been educated in these schools. This is an example of how government might interfere in the education of subjects, and how much evil might arise from compulsion.

People imagine, indeed, that experiments in education are unnecessary, and that we can judge from our reason whether anything is good or not. This is a great mistake, and experience teaches us that the results of an experiment are often entirely different from what we expected. Thus we see that, since we must be guided by experiments, no one generation can set forth a complete scheme of education. The only experimental school which had in a measure made a beginning to clear the way was the Dessau Institute. This must be said in its praise, in spite of the many mistakes with which we might reproach it—mistakes which attend all conclusions made from experiments—namely, that still more experiments are required.

This school was in a certain way the only one in which the teachers were free to work out their own methods and plans, and in which the teachers were in communication with each other and with all the learned men of Germany.[1]

21. Education includes the *nurture* of the child and, as it grows, its *culture*. The latter is firstly *negative*, consisting of discipline; that is, merely the correcting of faults. Secondly, culture is *positive*, consisting of instruction and guidance (and thus forming part of education). *Guidance* means directing the pupil in putting into practice what he has been taught. Hence the difference between a *private teacher* who merely instructs, and a *tutor* or *governor* who

[1] In the editions of Rink and Schubert § 27 follows here.—(Tr.) See p. 60.

guides and directs his pupil. The one trains for
school only, the other for life.

22. Education is either *private* or *public*.
The latter is concerned only with instruction,
and this can always remain public. The carrying out of what is taught is left to private
education. A complete public education is one
which unites instruction and moral culture.
Its aim is to promote a good private education.
A school which does this is called an educational
institute. There cannot be many such institutions, and the number of children in them can
be but small, since the fees must of necessity be
high, for the institutions require elaborate management, which entails a good deal of expense.
It is the same as with almshouses and hospitals.
The buildings required for them, and the
salaries of directors, overseers, and servants,
take away at once half of the funds, so that
there can be no doubt that the poor would be
better provided for, if all that money were sent
direct to their houses. For this reason it is
also difficult to provide that any but the children
of rich people should share in these institutions.

23. The object of such *public institutions* as
these is the improvement of home education.

If only parents, or those who are their fellow-helpers in the work of education, were well educated themselves, the expense of public institutions might be avoided. The purpose of these institutions is to make experiments, and to educate individuals, so that in time a good private education may arise out of these public institutions.

24. *Home education* is carried on either by the parents themselves, or, should the parents not have the time, aptitude, or inclination for it, by others who are paid to assist them in it. But in education which is carried on by these assistants one very great difficulty arises—namely, the division of authority between parent and teacher. The child is called upon to obey the teacher's rule, and at the same time to follow his parents' whims. The only way out of this difficulty is for the parents to surrender the whole of their authority to the tutor.

25. How far, then, has home education an advantage over public education, or *vice versâ*? Regarded not only from the point of view of developing ability, but also as a preparation for the duties of a citizen, it must, I am inclined to think, be allowed that, on the whole, public education is the best. Home education frequently not only fosters family failings, but tends to continue these failings in the new generation.

26. *How long*, then, should education *last*? Till the youth has reached that period of his life when nature has ordained that he shall be capable of guiding his own conduct; when the instinct of sex has developed in him, and he can become a father himself, and have to educate his own children. This period is generally reached about the sixteenth year. After this we may still make use of some means of culture, and secretly exercise some discipline; but of education in the ordinary sense of the word we shall have no further need.

27. In the first period of childhood the child must learn submission and positive [1] obedience. In the next stage he should be allowed to think for himself, and to enjoy a certain amount of freedom, although still obliged to follow certain rules. In the first period there is a mechanical, in the second a moral constraint.

28. The child's submission is either *positive* or *negative*. *Positive* in that he is obliged to do

---

[1] Rink and Schubert read: 'passive.'—(Tr.)

what he is told, because he cannot judge for himself, and the faculty of imitation is still strong in him; or *negative*, in that he is obliged to do what others wish him to do, if he wishes others to do him a good turn.[1] In the former case, the consequence of not obeying is punishment; in the latter, the fact that people do not comply with his wishes. He is in this case, though capable of thinking for himself, dependent on others with regard to his own pleasure.

29. One of the greatest problems of education is how to unite submission to the necessary *restraint* with the child's capability of exercising his *freewill*—for restraint is necessary. How am I to develop the sense of freedom in spite of the restraint? I am to accustom my pupil to endure a restraint of his freedom, and at the same time I am to guide him to use his freedom aright. Without this all education is merely mechanical, and the child, when his education is over, will never be able to make a proper use of his freedom. He should be made to feel early the inevitable

---

[1] Vogt's text is here obviously corrupt. The reading given is taken from the editions of Rink and Schubert.—(Tr.)

opposition of society, that he may learn how difficult it is to support himself, to endure privation, and to acquire those things which are necessary to make him independent.

30. Here we must observe the following : —

First, we must allow the child from his earliest childhood perfect liberty in every respect (except on those occasions when he might hurt himself—as, for instance, when he clutches at a knife), provided that in acting so he does not interfere with the liberty of others. For instance, as soon as he screams or is too boisterously happy, he annoys others.

Secondly, he must be shown that he can only attain his own ends by allowing others to attain theirs. For instance, should he be disobedient, or refuse to learn his lessons, he ought to be refused any treat he may have been looking forward to.

Thirdly, we must prove to him that restraint is only laid upon him that he may learn in time to use his liberty aright, and that his mind is being cultivated so that one day he may be free; that is, independent of the help of others. This is the last thing a child will come to understand. It is much later in life that children realise such facts as that they will afterwards have to support themselves; for they imagine that they can always go on as they are in their parents' house, and that food and drink will always be provided for them without any trouble on their part. Indeed, unless children, and especially the children of rich parents and princes, are made to realise this, they are like the inhabitants of Otaheiti, who remain children all their lives.

Again, we see the advantage of public education in that under such a system, we learn to measure our powers with those of others, and to know the limits imposed upon us by the rights of others. Thus we can have no preference shown us, because we meet with opposition everywhere, and we can only make our mark and obtain an advantage over others by real merit. Public education is the best school for future citizens.

There is yet another difficulty to be mentioned here—that is, the difficulty of anticipating the knowledge of sexual matters in such a manner as to prevent vice at the very outset of manhood. This, however, will be discussed later on.

31. Education is either *physical* or 'practical.' One part of physical education is that which man has in common with animals, namely, feeding and tending. '*Practical*' or *moral* training is that which teaches a man how to live as a free being. (We call anything '*practical*' which has reference to freedom.) This is the education of a personal character, of a free being, who is able to maintain himself, and to take his proper place in society, keeping at the same time a proper sense of his own individuality.

32. This '*practical*' education consists, then, of three parts :—

(*a*) The *ordinary curriculum of the school,* where the child's general ability is developed— the work of the schoolmaster.

(*b*) Instruction in the practical matters of life—to act with wisdom and discretion—the work of the private tutor or governess.

(*c*) The training of moral character.

Men need the training of school-teaching or instruction to develop the ability necessary to success in the various vocations of life. School-teaching bestows upon each member an individual value of his own.

Next, by learning the lesson of discretion in the practical matters of life, he is educated as a citizen, and becomes of value to his fellow-citizens, learning both how to accommodate himself to their society and also how to profit by it.

Lastly, moral training imparts to man a value with regard to the whole human race.

33. Of these three divisions of education school-teaching comes *first* in order of time; for a child's abilities must first be developed and trained, otherwise he is incapable of gaining knowledge in the practical matters of life. Discretion is the faculty of using our abilities aright.

Moral training, in as far as it is based upon fundamental principles which a man must himself comprehend, comes last in order of time. In so far, however, as it is based on common sense merely, it must be taken into account from the beginning, at the same time with physical training; for if moral training be omitted, many faults will take root in the child, against which all influences of education at a later stage will be powerless. As to ability and the general knowledge of life, everything must depend entirely upon the age of the pupil. Let a child be clever after the manner of children; let him be shrewd and good-natured in a childish way, but not cunning (*listig*) like a man. The latter is as unsuitable for a child as a childish mind is for a grown-up person.

CHAPTER II

34. ALTHOUGH those who undertake the home education of children do not have them entrusted to their care so early as to have charge of their physical education, at the same time it is useful for them to know all that is necessary to carry out this part of a child's education from first to last. Though the tutor may only have to do with older children, it may happen that others may be born in the house, and if he conducts himself wisely he will always have a claim to become the confidant of the parents, and to be consulted about the physical training of the little ones; the more so as often the tutor is the only well-educated person in the house. He should therefore have previously made himself acquainted with the subject of the physical education of children.

35. Physical training, properly speaking,

consists merely in the tending and feeding of the child, usually the work of parents or nurses.

The nourishment which Nature has provided for the infant is the mother's milk, and it is better for both when the mother is able to nurse her child. That the child's disposition is affected in this way, however, is mere prejudice, though one often hears it said of some trait of character : ‘You have imbibed that with your mother's milk.’

We must, however, make an exception in extreme cases, such as when the mother's condition is unhealthy. It was formerly believed that the first milk given by the mother after the birth of the infant, which resembles whey, is unwholesome, and must first be removed before the child is nursed.

Rousseau, however, called the attention of physicians to this point, to ascertain whether this first milk might not be useful to the child, since Nature has made nothing in vain, and it was actually found that the refuse which is always met with in a new-born child, which is known among doctors as *meconium*, is best removed by this milk, which is therefore useful and not harmful to the child.

36. The question has been asked whether an infant might not be as well brought up on the milk of animals; but human milk is very different in substance from the milk of animals. The milk of all those animals which live on grass and vegetables very soon curdles, if anything sour is added to it—tartaric acid, for instance, citric acid, or especially the acid of rennet. Human milk, on the other hand, does not curdle. But should the mother or nurse take a vegetable diet for a few days, her milk will curdle in the same way as cows' milk, &c.; though when she has returned to a meat diet for a little while, her milk will again become as good as ever. From this it has been concluded that it is best and most healthy for the mother or nurse to eat meat during the nursing period. When children throw up the milk, it is found to be curdled. The acid in the child's stomach must therefore accelerate the curdling of the milk more than any other kind of acid, since human milk cannot be brought to curdle in the ordinary way. How much worse would it be if milk were given to the child which curdled of itself! We see, however, from the customs of other nations with regard to the bringing up of their infants, that everything does not depend on this.

There is a certain tribe of Russians in Asia who eat scarcely anything but meat, and are a strong and healthy people. They are not, however, very long lived, and are of such a slight build that a full-grown youth, whom one would hardly expect to be so light, can be carried as easily as a child. On the other hand Swedes, and more particularly Indian nations, eat scarcely any meat, and yet their men are tall and well-formed. It seems, then, from these cases that all depends on the good health of the nurse, and that the best diet for mother or nurse is that which best agrees with her.

37. The question here arises as to how the child is to be fed if the mother's milk should cease. For some time past all sorts of farinaceous foods have been tried, but such food is not good for the child from the beginning.

We must especially bear in mind that nothing stimulating be given to the child, such as wine, spices, salt, &c. It is a singular fact, however, that children have such a strong craving for things of this sort ; this is because they act as a stimulant, and arouse their as yet undeveloped appetites in a manner pleasant to them. In Russia, it is true, children are given brandy to drink by their parents, who are great brandy-drinkers themselves, and it has been noticed that the Russians are a strong and healthy people. Certainly the fact of their being able to stand such a habit proves that they must have a good constitution : nevertheless, it is a fact that many who otherwise might have lived die in consequence of it. For such early stimulus to the nerves is the cause of many disorders. Children should be carefully kept even from too warm foods and drinks, as they are very apt to weaken the constitution.

38. Further we should notice that children need not be very warmly clad, for their blood is already naturally warmer than that of the full-grown. The heat of a child's blood reaches 110° Fahr., while the blood of a grown man or woman reaches only 96°. A child would be stifled in the same degree of warmth which his elders would enjoy. It is not good even for grown-up people to dress too warmly, to cover themselves up, and to accustom themselves to too warm drinks, for cool habits above all make people strong. Therefore it is good for a child to have

a cool and hard bed. Cold baths also are good. No stimulant must be allowed in order to excite the child's hunger, for hunger must only be the consequence of activity and occupation. However, the child must not be allowed so to accustom himself to anything as to feel the loss of it. It is better not to encourage artificially the formation of habits either good or bad.

39. Among savage nations the custom of swathing infants is never observed. Savage nations in America, for instance, make holes in the earth, and strew them with dust from rotting trees, which serves to keep the children to a certain extent clean and dry. In these holes the children lie, covered with leaves, having except for this covering, the free use of their limbs.

It is simply for the sake of our own convenience that we swathe our children like mummies, so that we may not have the trouble of watching them in order to prevent their limbs from getting broken or bent. And yet it often happens that they do get bent, just by swathing them. Also it makes the children themselves uneasy, and they are almost driven to despair on account of their never being able to use their limbs. And then people imagine that by calling to the child they stop its crying. But suppose a grown man were to be subjected to the same treatment, and we shall soon see whether he, too, would not cry and fall into uneasiness and despair.

In general we must bear in mind that early education is only negative—that is, we have not to add anything to the provision of Nature, but merely to see that such provision is duly carried out. If any addition to this is necessary on our part, it must be the process of hardening the child. For this reason, also, we must give up the habit of swathing our children. If, however, we want to use some kind of caution, the most suitable arrangement would be a kind of box covered with leather straps, such as the Italians use and call *arcuccio*. The child is never taken out of this box, even when nursed by its mother. This protects the child from the chance of being smothered when sleeping with its mother at night, while with us many children lose their lives in this way. This arrangement is better than swathing the child, since it allows greater freedom for the limbs, while at the same time it serves as a protection against anything that might hurt or bend its body.

40. Another custom belonging to early education is the rocking of babies. The easiest way of doing this is the way some peasants do it. The cradle is hung by a cord to the rafter, and, when the cord is pulled, the cradle rocks of itself from side to side. Rocking, however, is altogether objectionable, for the swinging backwards and forwards is bad for the child. We see this among grown people, in whom swinging often produces a feeling of sickness and giddiness. By swinging, nurses want to stun the child, so that he should not cry. But crying is a wholesome thing for a child, for when a child is born and draws its first breath the course of the blood in its veins is altered, which causes a painful sensation ; the child immediately cries, and the energy expended in crying develops and strengthens the various organs of its body. To run at once to a child's help when he cries—to sing to him, as the way of nurses is—is very bad for the child, and is often the beginning of spoiling him, for when he sees he gets things by crying for them he will cry all the more.[1]

41. Children are usually taught to walk by

[1] In the editions of Rink and Schubert §§ 51 and 48 follow here.—(Tr.)

means of leading-strings and go-carts; but, when one comes to think of it, it seems a surprising thing that people should insist upon teaching children how to walk, as if ever a human being had been found to be unable to walk for want of instruction. Besides, leading-strings are especially bad for the child. A writer once remarked that he had no doubt that the asthma from which he suffered was due to the use of leading-strings when he was a child, which he thought had narrowed his chest. For since a child takes hold of everything or picks up everything from the floor, his chest is confined by the leading-strings; and since the chest is still undeveloped, any pressure tends to flatten it, and the form it then takes is retained in after-life. Besides this, children do not learn to walk so surely as when they walk by themselves. The best plan is to let children crawl, until by degrees they learn of themselves to walk. To prevent them from hurting themselves with splinters from the floor, a woollen rug might be laid down, which would serve at the same time to break their fall.

It is commonly said that children fall very heavily; they do not, however; and it does

them no harm to fall sometimes. They learn
all the sooner to find their balance, and to fall
without hurting themselves.

It is customary to protect the child's head
with a kind of wide-brimmed bonnet, which is
supposed to prevent it from falling on its face.
But it is a merely negative education which
consists in employing artificial instruments,
instead of teaching the child to use those with
which Nature has already provided him. Here
the natural instruments are the child's hands,
which he will manage to use to steady himself.
The more artificial instruments we use, the more
do we become dependent on instruments.

42. Generally speaking, it would be better if
fewer instruments were used, and children were
allowed to learn more things by themselves.
They would then learn them more thoroughly.

For example, it is quite possible that a child
might learn to write by itself; for some one
must at one time have discovered this for
himself, and the discovery is not such a very
difficult one. For instance, if a child asked one
for bread, one might ask him to draw a picture
of what he wanted—he might then, perhaps,
draw a rough oval; on being asked to describe

his wants a little more accurately—for an oval might as well be a stone as a loaf—he might then be led on to express the letter B in some way, and so on. The child might invent his own alphabet in this way, which he would afterwards only have to exchange for other signs.

43. There are some children who come into the world with certain defects. Are there no means of remedying these defects? It has been decided, according to the opinion of many learned writers, that *stays* are of no use in such cases, but rather tend to aggravate the mischief by hindering the circulation of the blood and humours, and the healthy expansion of both the outer and inner parts of the body. If the child is left free he will exercise his body, and a man who has worn stays is weaker on leaving them off than a man who has never put them on. Perhaps some good might be done for those who are born crooked by more weight being put upon the side where the muscles are stronger. This, however, is a dangerous practice, too, for who is to decide what is the right balance?

It seems best that the child should learn to use his limbs, and remedy this defect by keeping his body in a certain position, even though he may find it troublesome, for no instruments are of any use in such cases.

44. All these artificial contrivances are the more hurtful in that they run counter to the aim of Nature in making organised and reasonable beings; for Nature requires them to keep their freedom, in order that they may learn how to use their powers. All that education can do in this matter is to prevent children from becoming *effeminate*. This might be done by accustoming them to habits of hardiness, which is the opposite of effeminacy. It is venturing too much to want to accustom children to everything. Russians have made the mistake of going too far in this direction, and consequently an enormous number of their children die young, from the over-hardening process. Habit is the result of the constant repetition of any one enjoyment or action, until such enjoyment or action becomes a necessity of our nature. There is nothing to which children become more easily accustomed, and which should be more carefully kept from them, than such highly stimulating things as tobacco, brandy, and warm drinks. Once acquired, it is very difficult to

give up these things; and giving them up causes
physical disturbances at first, since the repeated
use of anything effects a change in the functions
of the different organs of our body.   The more
habits a man allows himself to form, the less free
and independent he becomes; for it is the same
with man as with all other animals; whatever
he has been accustomed to early in life always
retains a certain attraction for him in after-life.
Children, therefore, must be prevented from
forming any habits, nor should habits be fostered
in them.

45. Many parents want to get their children
used to anything and everything.   But this is
no good.   For human nature in general, as well
as the nature of certain individuals in particular,
will not allow of such training, and consequently
many children remain apprentices all their lives.
Some parents, for instance, would have their
children go to sleep, get up, and have their
meals whenever they please; but in order that
they may do this with impunity, they must
follow a special diet, a diet which will strengthen
the body, and repair the evil which this irregu-
larity causes.   We find, indeed, many instances
of periodicity in Nature also.   Animals have

their appointed time to sleep, and man should accustom himself to a certain time, that the functions of the body be not disturbed. As to the other matter, that children ought to eat at any hour, we cannot well adduce here the case of the animal as an example; as, for instance, all grass-eating animals get but little nourishment each time they eat, therefore grazing is necessarily a constant occupation with them. It is, however, very important for man always to eat at regular hours. Many parents try to accustom their children to endure great cold, bad smells, and noises; this, however, is quite unnecessary, the only thing needful being to prevent them from forming habits. And for this it is best that they shall not always be subject to the same conditions.

46. A hard bed is much more healthy than a soft one; and, generally speaking, a severe education is very helpful in strengthening the body. By a severe education we must understand merely that which tends to prevent one from taking one's ease. Remarkable examples in confirmation of this assertion are not lacking, only they are not observed, or, to speak more correctly, people will not observe them.

47. With regard to the training of character —which we may indeed call also, in a certain sense, physical culture—we must chiefly bear in mind that *discipline* should not be slavish. For a child ought always to be conscious of his freedom, but always in such a way as not to interfere with the liberty of others—in which case he must be met with opposition. Many parents refuse their children everything they ask, in order that they may exercise their patience, but in doing so they require from their children more patience than they have themselves. This is cruel. One ought rather to give a child as much as will agree with him, and then tell him ' that is enough ' ; but this decision must be absolutely final. No attention should ever be given to a child when he cries for anything, and children's wishes should never be complied with if they try to extort something by crying; but if they ask properly, it should be given them, provided it is for their good. By this the child will also become accustomed to being open-minded ; and since he does not annoy anyone by his crying, everybody will be friendly towards him.

Providence seems indeed to have given

children happy, winning ways, in order that they may gain people's hearts. Nothing does children more harm than to exercise a vexatious and slavish discipline over them with a view to breaking their self-will.

48. During the first eight [1] months of a child's life its sense of sight is not fully developed. It experiences, it is true, the sensation of light, but cannot as yet distinguish one object from another. To convince ourselves of this, we have only to hold up a glittering object before the child's eyes and then remove it; we may at once notice that he does not follow it with his eyes.

At the same time as the sense of sight, the power of laughing and crying is developed. When the child has once reached that stage, *there is always some reasoning*, however vague it may be, *connected with his crying*. He cries with the idea that some harm has been done him. Rousseau says that if you merely tap a child of six months on the hand, it will scream as if a bit of burning wood had touched it. Here the child has actually a sense of grievance besides the mere bodily hurt. Parents talk a great deal

---

[1] Rink and Schubert read: 'three.'—(Tr.)

about breaking the will of their children, but there is no need to break their will unless they have already been spoilt. The spoiling begins when a child has but to cry to get his own way. It is very difficult to repair this evil later on; indeed, it can scarcely be done. We may keep the child from crying or otherwise worrying us, but he swallows his vexation, and is inwardly nursing anger all the more. In this way the child becomes accustomed to dissembling and agitation of mind. It is, for instance, very strange that parents should expect their children to turn and kiss their hand (*vide* p. 89) after they have just beaten them. That is the way to teach them dissembling and falsehood. For the child surely does not look on the rod with any special favour, so that he should feel any gratitude for its chastisement, and one can easily imagine with what feelings the child kisses the hand which has punished him.

49. We often say to a child: '*Fie, for shame!* you shouldn't do that,' &c. But such expressions are futile in this early stage of education; for the child has, as yet, no sense of shame or of seemliness. He has nothing to be ashamed of, and ought not to be ashamed.

These expressions therefore will simply make him timid. He will become embarrassed before others, and inclined to keep away from their company—and from this arises reserve and harmful concealment. He is afraid to ask for anything, when he ought to ask for all he wants. He conceals his true character, and always appears to be other than he is, when he ought to be able to speak frankly and freely. Instead of being always near his parents he shuns them, preferring to make friends with the servants of the house.

50. No better than this vexatious system of bringing up children is that of perpetually *playing with* and *caressing* the child ; this makes him self-willed and deceitful, and by betraying to him their weakness, parents lose the necessary respect in the eyes of the child. If, on the other hand, he is so trained that he gets nothing by crying for it, he will be frank without being bold, and modest without being timid. *Boldness*, or, what is almost the same thing, *insolence*, is insufferable. There are many men whose constant insolence has given them such an expression that their very look leads one to expect rudeness from them, while you have

only to look at others to see at once that they are incapable of being rude to anyone. Now we can always be frank in our demeanour, provided our frankness be united with a certain kindness. People often speak of men of rank having a royal air, but this is nothing but a certain self-sufficient manner in consequence of having met with no opposition all their life.[1]

51. It may be said with truth that the children of the *working classes* are more spoilt than the children of those of *higher rank*, for the working classes play with their children like monkeys, singing to them, caressing, kissing, and dancing with them. They think indeed they are doing a kindness to their child in always running to him when he cries, and playing with him, &c.; but he only cries the oftener. If, on the other hand, no notice is taken of the child's crying, he will leave off at last—for no one cares to continue a fruitless task. Once a child has become accustomed to having all his whims gratified, it is afterwards too late to begin to cross his will. On the other hand, if you do not mind the child's crying, he

[1] In the editions of Rink and Schubert §§ 57, 58, and 59 follow here.—(Tr.)

will soon get tired of it. But should his fancies always be gratified, both his character and his manners will be spoilt.

The child has as yet, indeed, no idea of manners, but it goes far towards spoiling his natural disposition, so that afterwards sharp measures are necessary to undo the evil caused by early indulgence. When attempts are made later on to break off the habit of giving way to all the child's wishes, his crying is then accompanied by a rage as fierce as any of which grown-up people are capable, only that he has not the physical strength to exercise it. This is but what we must expect, for children who have been for so long accustomed merely to cry to get what they want, become veritable despots, and are naturally aggrieved when their rule comes suddenly to an end; for even grown-up people who have been for some time in a high position find it very difficult if they are suddenly called upon to abdicate.

52. Here we have also to discuss the training of the *sense of pleasure* or *pain*. In this our work must be negative; we must see that the child's sensibility be not spoilt by over-indulgence. Love of ease does more harm than all

the ills of life. Therefore it is of the utmost importance that children should be taught early to work. If they have not been over-indulged, children are naturally fond of amusements which are attended with fatigue, and occupations which require exercise of strength. With regard to pleasures, it is best not to let them be dainty, nor to allow them to pick and choose. As a rule, mothers spoil their children in this way and indulge them altogether too much. In spite of this we very often notice that children, and especially boys, are fonder of their father than of their mother. This is probably because mothers are timid, and do not allow them to use their limbs as freely as they would wish, for fear of the children hurting themselves. While fathers, on the other hand, although they are stern to them, and perhaps punish them severely when they are naughty, yet take them out sometimes into the fields and do not try to hinder their boyish games.

53. Some people believe that in making children wait a long time for what they want they teach them *patience*. This is, however, hardly necessary, though doubtless in times of illness, &c., patience is needed. Patience is two-fold, consisting either in giving up all hope or in gaining new courage to go on. The first is not necessary, provided what we hope to gain is possible; the second we should always desire, as long as what we strive for is right. In cases of illness, however, hopelessness spoils what has been made good by cheerfulness. But he who is still capable of taking courage with regard to his physical or moral condition is not likely to give up all hope.[1]

54. The *will* of children, as has been already remarked, must not be broken, but merely bent in such a way that it may yield to natural

[1] In the editions of Rink and Schubert the following is here inserted:

' Children should not be intimidated. This happens particularly when they are addressed in terms of abuse, and are often put to shame. A case in point is the exclamation made use of by many parents: " Fie, for shame! " It is not at all clear why children should be ashamed of themselves for sucking their fingers and things of that kind. They may be told that it is not customary to do so, or that it is not good manners. But only in the case of lying ought they to be told to be ashamed of what they have done. Nature has bestowed the feeling of shame on man in order that self-betrayal may immediately follow upon lying. Hence, if parents do not arouse shame in their children, except when they have lied, this feeling of shame with regard to untruth will endure all their lifetime. If, however, they are constantly put to shame, there is produced a kind of bashfulness from which they can never subsequently free themselves.'—(Tr.)

obstacles. At the beginning, it is true, the child must obey blindly. It is unnatural that a child should command by his crying, and that the strong should obey the weak. Children should never, even in their earliest childhood, be humoured because they cry, nor allowed to extort anything by crying. Parents often make a mistake in this, and then, wishing to undo the result of their over-indulgence, they deny their children in later life whatever they ask for. It is, however, very wrong to refuse them without cause what they may naturally expect from the kindness of their parents, merely for the sake of opposing them, and that they, being the weaker, should bo made to feel the superior power of their parents.

55. To grant children their wishes is to *spoil* them ; to thwart them purposely is an utterly *wrong way of bringing them up.* The former generally happens as long as they are the playthings of their parents, and especially during the time when they are beginning to talk. By spoiling a child, however, very great harm is done, affecting its whole life. Those who thwart the wishes of children prevent them (and must necessarily prevent them) at the same time from showing their anger ; but their inward rage will be all the stronger, for children have not yet learned to control themselves.

The following rules should accordingly be observed with children from their earliest days :— When they cry, and we have reason to believe they are hurt, we should go to their help. On the other hand, when they cry simply from temper, they should be left alone. And this way of dealing with them should be continued as they grow older. In this case the opposition the child meets with is quite natural, and, properly speaking, merely negative, consisting simply in his not being indulged. Many children, on the other hand, get all they want from their parents by persistent asking. If children are allowed to get whatever they want by crying, they become ill-tempered ; while if they are allowed to get whatever they want by asking, their characters are weakened. Should there, then, be no important reason to the contrary, a child's request should be granted ; should there be a reason to the contrary, it should not be granted, no matter how often the request is repeated. A refusal should always be final.

This will shortly have the effect of making its repetition unnecessary.

56. Supposing—what is of extremely rare occurrence—that a child should be naturally inclined to be *stubborn*, it is best to deal with him in this way :—If he refuses to do anything to please us, we must refuse to do anything to please him.

Breaking a child's will makes him a slave, while natural opposition makes him docile.

57. All this we may consider as negative training, for many weaknesses of mankind proceed not so much from lack of teaching as from *false impressions.* For instance, fear of spiders and toads, &c., is suggested to children by their nurses. A child would probably pick up a spider as readily as anything else, were it not that the nurse's horror at the sight of spiders has affected the child by a sort of sympathy. Many children retain this fear all their lives, and in this matter always remain childish ; for spiders, though dangerous to flies, for whom their bite is poisonous, are harmless to men. In the same way the toad is as harmless as the beautiful green frog or any other animal.

CHAPTER III

58. THE positive part of physical education is *culture*. It is this which distinguishes man from the animals. Culture consists chiefly in the exercise of the mental faculties. Parents, then, should give their children opportunities for such exercise. The first and most important rule is that all artificial aids should, as far as possible, be dispensed with. Thus in early childhood leading-strings and go-carts should be discarded, and the child allowed to crawl about on the ground till he learns to go by himself— he will then walk more steadily. For the use of tools is the ruin of natural quickness. Thus we want a cord to measure a certain distance, though we might as well measure it by the eye; or a clock to tell the time, when we might do this by the position of the sun; or a compass to find our way in a forest, when we might

instead be guided by the position of the sun by
day, of the stars by night.   Indeed, we might
even say that instead of needing a boat we
might swim across the water.   The celebrated
Franklin wondered why everyone didn't learn
to swim, since swimming is so pleasant and so
useful.   He also suggested an easy way by which
to teach oneself to swim :—Standing in a brook
with the water up to your neck, you drop an
egg into the water, and then try to reach it.   In
bending forward to do this you will be carried
off your feet, and, in order to prevent the water
getting into your mouth, you will throw your
head back.   You are now in the proper position for swimming, and have only to strike out
with the arms to find yourself actually swimming.

What has to be done is to see that natural
ability is cultivated.   Sometimes instruction
is necessary; sometimes the child's mind is
inventive enough, or he invents tools for
himself.

59. What should be observed in physical
education, with respect to the training of the
body, relates either to the use of voluntary
movements or to the organs of sense.   As to

the first of these, what is wanted is that the
child should always help himself. For this,
both strength and skill, quickness and self-confidence, are necessary, so as to be able, for
instance, to go along narrow paths, or to climb
steep places with an abyss before one's eye, or
to cross a slender plank. If a man cannot do
this, he is not entirely what he might be.

Since the *Philanthropinon* [1] of Dessau set the
example, many attempts of this kind have been
made with children in other institutions. It is
wonderful to read how the Swiss accustom themselves from early childhood to climb mountains,
how readily they venture along the narrowest
paths with perfect confidence, and leap over
chasms, having first measured the distance with
the eye, lest it should prove to be beyond their
powers.

Most people, however, fear some imaginary
danger of falling, and this fear actually paralyses
their limbs, so that for them such a proceeding
would be really fraught with danger. This fear
generally grows with age, and is chiefly found

[1] This refers to the Philanthropist schools founded in
Germany in and after 1774, of which the above-mentioned
was the first.—(Tr.)

in those men who work much with their heads.
For children to make such attempts is not
really very dangerous; they are much lighter
in proportion to their strength than grown-up
people, and for this reason do not fall so heavily.
Besides this, their bones are not so inflexible and
brittle as they become with age. Children often
put their strength to the proof of their own
accord. We often see them climbing, for instance, for no particular reason. Running is
a healthy exercise and strengthens the body.
Jumping, lifting weights, carrying, slinging,
throwing towards a mark, wrestling, running
races, and all such exercises are good. Dancing,
so far as it is of an elaborate kind, is not so
well suited to actual childhood.

60. Exercises in throwing, whether it be
throwing a distance or hitting a mark, have the
additional advantage of exercising the *senses*,
especially the eyesight. Games with balls are
among the best for children, as they necessitate
healthy running.

Generally speaking, those games are the best
which unite the development of skill with the
exercise of the senses—for example, those that
exercise the eyesight in correctly judging dis-

tance, size and proportion, in finding the position
of places in different regions by means of the
sun, &c.   All these are good training.   Of great
advantage also is local imagination, by which
we mean the capability [1] of recalling the exact
position of places where we have seen certain
things—as, for example, when we are able to
find our way out of a forest by having noticed
the trees we have passed.   In the same way the
memoria localis,[2] by which we recall, not only in
what book we have read a certain thing, but in
what part of the book.   Thus the musician has
the keys before his mind's eye, and does not
need to have the actual instrument before him
while he composes.   It is very useful also to
cultivate the ear of children, so that they may
know whether a sound comes from far or near,
from this side or that.

61. The children's game of ' blindman's buff '
was already known among the Greeks, who
called it μυΐνδα.   Generally speaking, children's
games are the same everywhere; those which
are found in Germany being also found in
France and England, and so on.   They have

---

[1] Rink and Schubert read : ' pleasure.'—(Tr.)
[2] Memory for places.

their principle in a certain instinct common to all children. In ' blindman's buff,' for instance, there is the desire to know how they would help themselves were they deprived of one of their senses.

Spinning tops is a singular game. Such games as these furnish matter for further reflection to grown-up men, and occasionally lead even to important discoveries. Thus Segner has written a treatise on the top ; and the top has furnished an English sea-captain with material for inventing a mirror, by means of which the height of the stars may be measured from a ship.

Children are fond of noisy instruments, such as trumpets, drums, and the like ; but these are objectionable, since they become a nuisance to others. It would be less objectionable, however, were children to learn how to cut a reed so as to play on it.

Swinging is also a healthy exercise, as well for grown-up people as for children. Children, however, should be watched, lest they swing too fast.

Kite-flying is also an unobjectionable game. It calls forth skill, the flight of the kite depending on its being in a certain position relatively to the wind.

62. For the sake of these games the boy will deny himself in his other wants, and thus train himself unconsciously for other and greater privations. Further, he will accustom himself to constant occupation; nevertheless for that very reason these games must not be mere games, but games having some end and object. For the more a child's body is strengthened and hardened in this way, the more surely will he be saved from the ruinous consequences of over-indulgence. Gymnastics also are intended merely to direct Nature; hence we must not aim at artificial grace.

Discipline must precede instruction. Here, however, in training the bodies of children we must also take care to fit them for society. Rousseau says: 'You will never get an able man, unless you have a street urchin first.' A lively boy will sooner become a good man than a conceited and priggish lad.

A child must learn to be neither troublesome nor insinuating in company. He must be confident at the invitation of others without being obtrusive, and frank without being impertinent. As a means to this end all we have to do is not to spoil the child's nature, either by giving him such ideas of good behaviour as will only serve to make him timid and shy, or, on the other hand, by suggesting to him a wish to assert himself. Nothing is more ridiculous than precocious good behaviour and priggish self-conceit in a child. In this last instance we must let the child see his weakness all the more, but at the same time we must not overpower him with a sense of our own superiority and power ; so that, though the child may develop his own individuality, he should do so only as a member of society—in a world which must, it is true, be large enough for him, but also for others. Toby in ‘ Tristram Shandy ’ says to a fly which has been annoying him for some time, and which he at last puts out of the window, ‘ Go away, tiresome creature ; the world is large enough for us both.’ We may each of us take these words for our motto. We need not be troublesome to one another ; the world is large enough for all of us.

CHAPTER IV

63. WE come now to the *cultivation of the mind*, which also we may call, in a certain sense, physical. We must, however, distinguish between nature and freedom. To give laws to freedom is quite another thing to cultivating nature. The nature of the body and the nature of the mind agree in this, that culture goes to prevent the spoiling of either, and that art adds something to both. We may, therefore, call the cultivation of the mind physical, in a certain sense, just as well as the cultivation of the body.

This physical cultivation of the mind, however, must be distinguished from moral training, in that it aims only at nature, while moral training aims at freedom. A man may be highly cultivated physically, he may have a well-cultivated mind; but if he lacks moral culture, he will be a wicked man.

Physical culture must, however, be distinguished from '*practical*' culture, which last is *pragmatic* or *moral*. In this last case *morality* is the aim rather than *culture*.

64. The *physical* cultivation of the mind may be divided into (i) *free* and (ii) *scholastic* culture. Free culture is, as it were, but a pastime, while scholastic culture constitutes a business. Free culture is that which must always be observed with the child. In scholastic culture, on the other hand, the child is looked upon as under restraint. We may be occupied in games, which we call being occupied in our leisure time, and we may be occupied by compulsion, which we call work. Scholastic culture constitutes *work* for the child, free culture constitutes *play*.

65. Various plans of education have been drawn up by different people, in order to discover the best methods—a most praiseworthy undertaking. One among others suggests that children should be allowed to *learn everything as it were in play*. In an article in the ' Göttingen Magazine ' Lichtenberg ridicules the folly of trying to make everything like play for boys,

while they ought to be accustomed to serious
business at an early period, since they must
some time enter a business life. This is an
utterly preposterous notion. A child must play,
must have his hours of recreation ; but he must
also learn to work. It is a good thing, doubtless,
to exercise skill, as it is to cultivate the mind, but
these two kinds of culture should have their
separate hours. Moreover, it is a great misfortune for man that he is by nature so inclined to
inaction. The longer a man gives way to this
inclination, the more difficult will he find it to
make up his mind to work.

66. In *work* the occupation is not pleasant
in itself, but it is undertaken for the sake of the
end in view. In *games*, on the other hand, the
occupation is pleasant in itself without having
any other end in view. When we go for a walk,
we do so for the sake of the walk, and therefore
the further we go the pleasanter it is ; while
when we go to a certain place, our object is the
company which we shall find there, or something
else, and therefore we shall naturally choose the
shortest way. The same thing happens in card
games. It is really extraordinary how reasonable
men can sit by the hour and shuffle cards. It

is not, it seems, so easy for men to leave off being children. For how is this a better game than the children's game of ball? It is true that grown men do not care to ride hobby-horses, but they ride other hobbies.

67. It is of the greatest importance that children should learn to work. Man is the only animal who is obliged to work. He must go through a long apprenticeship before he can enjoy anything for his own sustenance. The question whether Heaven would not have shown us greater kindness by supplying all our wants without the necessity of work on our part must certainly be answered in the negative, for man needs occupation, even occupation that involves a certain amount of restraint. Just as false a notion is it that if Adam and Eve had only remained in Paradise they would have done nothing there but sit together singing pastoral songs and admiring the beauty of Nature. Were this so, they would have been tormented with *ennui*, just as much as other people in the same position.

Men ought to be occupied in such a way that, filled with the idea of the end which they have before their eyes, they are not conscious of themselves, and the best rest for them is the rest which follows work. In the same way a child must become accustomed to work, and where can the inclination to work be cultivated so well as at school? School is a place of compulsory culture. It is very bad for a child to learn to look upon everything as play. He must, it is true, have his time for recreation, but he must also have his time for work. Even though the child does not at once understand the use of this restraint, later in life he will recognise its value. It would be merely training the child to bad habits of inquisitiveness were one always to answer his questions : ' What is the use of this ? ' or, ' What is the use of that ? ' Education must be compulsory, but it need not therefore be slavish.

68. With regard to the '*free*' [1] cultivation of the *mental faculties*, we must remember that this cultivation is going on constantly. It really deals with the superior faculties. The inferior faculties must be cultivated along with them, but only with a view to the superior ; for instance, the intelligence with a view to the understanding—the principal rule that we should follow being that no mental faculty is to

[1] Vogt omits the word ' free ' here.—(Tr.)

be cultivated by itself, but always in relation to others; for instance, the imagination to the advantage of the understanding.

The inferior faculties have no value in themselves; for instance, a man who has a good memory, but no judgment. Such a man is merely a walking dictionary. These beasts of burden of Parnassus are of some use, however, for if they cannot do anything useful themselves they at least furnish material out of which others may produce something good. Intelligence divorced from judgment produces nothing but foolishness. Understanding is the knowledge of the general. Judgment is the application of the general to the particular. Reason is the power of understanding the connection between the general and the particular. This free culture runs its course from childhood onwards till the time that the young man is released from all education. When a young man, for instance, quotes a general rule, we may make him quote examples drawn from history or fable in which this rule is disguised, passages from the poets where it is expressed, and thus encourage him to exercise both his intelligence and his memory, &c.

69. The maxim *Tantum scimus, quantum memoria tenemus* [1] is quite true—hence it is very necessary to cultivate the memory. Things are so constituted that the understanding first follows the mental impression, and the memory must preserve this impression. So it is, for instance, in languages. We learn them either by the formal method of committing them to memory or by conversation—this last being the best method for modern languages. The learning of words is really necessary, but the best plan is for the youth to learn words as he comes across them in the author he is reading. The youth should have a certain set task. In the same way geography is best learnt mechanically. What is learnt in a mechanical way is best retained by the memory, and in a great many cases this way is indeed very useful. The proper mechanism for the study of history has yet to be found. An attempt has been made in this direction consisting of a system of tables, but the result has not been very satisfactory. History, however, is an excellent means of exercising the understanding in judging rightly. Learning by heart is very necessary, but doing it merely for

[1] We know just so much as we remember.

the sake of exercising the memory is of no use educationally—for instance, the learning of a speech by heart. At all events, it only serves to encourage forwardness. Besides this, declamation is only proper for grown-up men. The same may be said of all those things which we learn merely for some future examination or with a view to *futuram oblivionem.*[1] The memory should only be occupied with such things as are important to be retained, and which will be of service to us in real life. Novel-reading is the worst thing for children, since they can make no further use of it, and it merely affords them entertainment for the moment. Novel-reading weakens the memory. For it would be ridiculous to remember novels in order to relate them to others. Therefore all novels should be taken away from children. Whilst reading them they weave, as it were, an inner romance of their own, rearranging the circumstances for themselves ; their fancy is thus imprisoned, but there is no exercise of thought.

Distractions must never be allowed, least of all in school, for the result will be a certain propensity in that direction which might soon

[1] Future forgetfulness.

grow into a habit. Even the finest talents may be wasted when once a man is subject to distraction. Although children are inattentive at their games, they soon recall their attention. We may notice, however, that they are most distracted when they are thinking of some mischief, for then they are contriving either how to hide it, or else how to repair the evil done. They then only half hear anything, give wrong answers, and know nothing about what they are reading, &c.

70. The memory must be cultivated early, but we must be careful to cultivate the understanding at the same time.

The memory is cultivated (i) by learning the names which are met with in tales, (ii) by reading and writing. But as to reading, children should practise it with the head, without depending on the spelling. (iii) By languages, which children should first learn by hearing, before they read anything.

Then a well-constructed so-called *orbis pictus* will prove very useful. We might begin with botany, mineralogy, and natural history in general. In order to make sketches of these objects, drawing and modelling will have to be learned, and for this some knowledge of mathematics is necessary. The first lessons in science will most advantageously be directed to the study of geography, mathematical as well as physical. Tales of travel, illustrated by pictures and maps, will lead on to political geography. From the present condition of the earth's surface we go back to its earlier condition, and this leads us to ancient geography, ancient history, and so on.

But in teaching children we must seek insensibly to unite knowledge with the carrying out of that knowledge into practice. Of all the sciences, mathematics seems to be the one that best fulfils this. Further, knowledge and speech (ease in speaking, fluency, eloquence) must be united. The child, however, must learn also to distinguish clearly between knowledge and mere opinion and belief. Thus we prepare the way for a right understanding, and a *right*—not a *refined* or *delicate*—taste. This taste must at first be that of the senses, especially the eyes, but ultimately of ideas.

71. It is necessary to have rules for everything which is intended to cultivate the understanding. It is very useful mentally to separate the rules, that the understanding may proceed not merely

mechanically, but with the consciousness of following a rule.

It is also very useful to bring these rules into a set form, and thus commit them to memory. If we keep the rule in our memory, though we forget its application, we shall soon find our way again.

Here the question arises whether the rules shall first be studied *in abstracto*, and whether they ought to be studied after they have been applied, or whether the rule and its application should be studied side by side. This last is the only advisable course; otherwise the application of the rule is very uncertain till the rule itself is learned.

But from time to time the rules must also be arranged in classes, for it is difficult to keep them in memory when they are not associated together. Consequently in learning languages the study of grammar must always, to a certain extent, come first.

72. We must now give a systematic idea of the whole aim of education, and the means of obtaining it.

I. *The general cultivation of the mental faculties, as distinguished from the cultivation of*

particular mental faculties.—This aims at skill
and perfection, and has not for its object
the imparting of any particular knowledge,
but the general strengthening of the mental
faculties.

This culture is either (*a*) *physical*—here everything depends upon exercise and discipline,
without the child needing to learn any 'maxims';
it is passive for the pupil, who has only to follow
the guidance of others—or (*b*) it is moral. This
depends not upon discipline, but upon 'maxims.'[1]
All will be spoilt if moral training rests upon
examples, threats, punishments, and so on. It
would then be merely discipline. We must see
that the child does right on account of his own
'maxims,' and not merely from habit; and not
only that he does right, but that he does it
because it is right. For the whole moral value
of actions consists in 'maxims' concerning the
good.

Physical education, then, is distinguished
from moral in the former being passive, while
the latter is active, for the child. He should

---

[1] 'Maxim' is an important term in Kant's *Moral Philo-
sophy*, and by it must be understood general principles of right
and wrong.—(Tr.)

always understand the principle of an action, and its relation to the idea of duty.

73. II. *The cultivation of particular mental faculties.*—This includes the cultivation of the faculty of cognition, of the senses, the imagination, memory, power of attention, and intelligence—in a word, the inferior powers of the understanding.

Of the cultivation of the senses—eyesight, for instance—we have already spoken. As to the cultivation of the imagination, the following is to be noticed:—Children generally have a very lively imagination, which does not need to be expanded or made more intense by the reading of fairy tales. It needs rather to be curbed and brought under rule, but at the same time should not be left quite unoccupied. There is something in maps which attracts everybody, even the smallest children. When they are tired of everything else, they will still learn something by means of maps. And this is a good amusement for children, for here their imagination is not allowed to rove, since it must, as it were, confine itself to certain figures. We might really begin with geography in teaching children. Figures of animals, plants, and so on, might be added at the same time; these will make the study of geography more lively. History, however, would probably have to come later on.

With regard to the power of attention, we may remark that this faculty needs general strengthening. The power of rigidly fixing our thoughts upon one object is not so much a talent as a weakness of our mind, which in this case is inflexible, and does not allow itself to be applied at pleasure. But distraction is the enemy of all education. Memory depends upon our attention.

74. As regards the cultivation of the *superior mental faculties*, this includes the cultivation of the understanding, judgment, and reason. The understanding may at first be cultivated, in a certain way, passively also, either by quoting examples which prove the rules, or, on the contrary, by discovering rules for particular cases. The judgment shows us what use to make of the understanding. Understanding is necessary in order that we may understand what we learn or say, and that we may not repeat anything without understanding it. How many people hear and read things which

they do not understand, though they believe them! Of that kind are both images and real things.

It is through reason that we get an insight into principles. But we must remember that we are speaking here of a reason which still needs guidance. Hence the child should not be encouraged to be always reasoning, nor should we indulge in reasoning in the presence of children, about things which surpass their conception.

We are not dealing here with speculative reason, but only with reflection upon actual occurrences, according to their causes and effects. It is in its arrangement and working a practical reason.

75. The best way of cultivating the mental faculties is to *do ourselves* all that we wish to accomplish ; for instance, by carrying out into practice the grammatical rule which we have learnt. We understand a map best when we are able to draw it out for ourselves. The best way to understand is to do. That which we learn most thoroughly, and remember the best, is what we have in a way taught ourselves. There are but few men, however, who are capable of

doing this. They are called self-taught (αὐτο-
δίδακτοι).

76. In the culture of *reason* we must proceed
according to the Socratic method. Socrates,
who called himself the midwife of his hearers'
knowledge, gives examples in his dialogues,
which Plato has in a manner preserved for us,
of the way in which, even in the case of grown-
up people, ideas may be drawn forth from their
own individual reason. In many respects
children need not exercise their reason. They
must not be allowed to argue about everything.
It is not necessary for them to know the
principles of everything connected with their
education ; but when the question of duty arises,
they should be made to understand those
principles. But on the whole we should try to
draw out their own ideas, founded on reason,
rather than to introduce such ideas into their
minds. The Socratic method should form, then,
the rule for the catechetical method. True it is
somewhat slow, and it is difficult to manage so
that in drawing ideas out of one child the others
shall also learn something. The mechanical
method of catechising is also useful in some
sciences ; for instance, in the explanation of

revealed religion. In universal religion, on the other hand, we must employ the Socratic method. As to what has to be learnt historically, the mechanical method of catechising is much to be commended.

CHAPTER V

MORAL CULTURE

77. *MORAL CULTURE* must be based upon
'maxims,' not upon discipline ; the one prevents
evil habits, the other trains the mind to think.
We must see, then, that the child should accustom himself to act in accordance with
'maxims,' and not from certain over-changing
springs of action. Through discipline we form
certain habits, moreover, the force of which
becomes lessened in the course of years. The
child should learn to act according to 'maxims,'
the reasonableness of which he is able to see for
himself. One can easily see that there is some
difficulty in carrying out this principle with
young children, and that moral culture demands
a great deal of insight on the part of parents and
teachers.

Supposing a child tells a lie, for instance, he
ought not to be punished, but treated with con-

tempt, and told that he will not be believed in the future, and the like. If you punish a child for being naughty, and reward him for being good, he will do right merely for the sake of the reward; and when he goes out into the world and finds that goodness is not always rewarded, nor wickedness always punished, he will grow into a man who only thinks about how he may get on in the world, and does right or wrong according as he finds either of advantage to himself.

78. ' *Maxims* ' ought to originate in the human being as such. In moral training we should seek early to infuse into children ideas as to what is right and wrong. If we wish to establish morality, we must abolish punishment. Morality is something so sacred and sublime that we must not degrade it by placing it in the same rank as discipline. The first endeavour in moral education is the formation of character. Character consists in readiness to act in accordance with 'maxims.' At first they are school ' maxims,' and later ' maxims ' of mankind. At first the child obeys rules. ' Maxims ' are also rules, but subjective rules. They proceed from the understanding of man. No infringement of school discipline must be allowed to go unpunished, although the punishment must always fit the offence.

79. If we wish to *form the characters* of children, it is of the greatest importance to point out to them a certain plan, and certain rules, in everything; and these must be strictly adhered to. For instance, they must have set times for sleep, for work, and for pleasure; and these times must be neither shortened nor lengthened. With indifferent matters children might be allowed to choose for themselves, but having once made a rule they must always follow it. We must, however, form in children the character of a child, and not the character of a citizen.

Unmethodical men are not to be relied on; it is difficult to understand them, and to know how far we are to trust them. It is true we often blame people who always act by rule—for instance, the man who does everything by the clock, having a fixed hour for every one of his actions—but we blame them often unreasonably, for this exactness, though it looks like pedantry, goes far towards helping the formation of character.

80. Above all things, obedience is an essen-

tial feature in the character of a child, especially
of a school boy or girl. This obedience is twofold,
including absolute obedience to his master's
commands, and obedience to what he feels to be
a good and reasonable will. Obedience may be
the result of compulsion ; it is then *absolute* : or
it may arise out of confidence ; it is then obedience of the second kind. This *voluntary* obedience is very important, but the former is also
very necessary, for it prepares the child for the
fulfilment of laws that he will have to obey later,
as a citizen, even though he may not like them.

81. Children, then, must be subject to a certain law of *necessity*. This law, however, must
be a general one—a rule which has to be kept
constantly in view, especially in schools. The
master must not show any predilection or
preference for one child above others ; for thus
the law would cease to be general. As soon as
a child sees that the other children are not all
placed under the same rules as himself, he will
at once become refractory.

82. One often hears it said that we should
put everything before children in such a way
that they shall do it from *inclination*. In some
cases, it is true, this is all very well, but

there is much besides which we must place before them as *duty*. And this will be of great use to them throughout their life. For in the paying of rates and taxes, in the work of the office, and in many other cases, we must be led, not by inclination, but by duty. Even though a child should not be able to see the reason of a duty, it is nevertheless better that certain things should be prescribed to him in this way; for, after all, a child will always be able to see that he has certain duties as a child, while it will be more difficult for him to see that he has certain duties as a human being. Were he able to understand this also—which, however, will only be possible in the course of years—his obedience would be still more perfect.

83. Every transgression of a command in a child is a want of obedience, and this brings *punishment* with it. Also, should a command be disobeyed through inattention, punishment is still necessary. This punishment is either *physical* or *moral*. It is *moral* when we do something derogatory to the child's longing to be honoured and loved (a longing which is an aid to moral training); for instance, when we humiliate the child by treating him coldly and distantly. This longing of children should, however, be cultivated as much as possible. Hence this kind of punishment is the best, since it is an aid to moral training—for instance, if a child tells a lie, a look of contempt is punishment enough, and punishment of a most appropriate kind.

Physical punishment consists either in refusing a child's requests or in the infliction of pain. The first is akin to moral punishment, and is of a negative kind. The second form must be used with caution, lest an *indoles servilis*[1] should be the result. It is of no use to give children rewards ; this makes them selfish, and gives rise to an *indoles mercenaria*.[2]

84. Further, obedience is either that of the child or that of the *youth*. Disobedience is always followed by punishment. This is either a really *natural* punishment, which a man brings upon himself by his own behaviour—for instance, when a child gets ill from over-eating—and this kind of punishment is the best, since a man is subject to it throughout his life, and not merely during his childhood ; or, on the other hand, the

---

[1] A slavish disposition.
[2] The disposition of a hireling.

punishment is artificial. By taking into consideration the child's desire to be loved and respected, such punishments may be chosen as will have a lasting effect upon its character. Physical punishments must merely supplement the insufficiency of moral punishment. If moral punishment have no effect at all, and we have at last to resort to physical punishment, we shall find after all that no good character is formed in this way. At the beginning, however, physical restraint may serve to take the place of reflection.

85. Punishments inflicted with signs of *anger* are useless. Children then look upon the punishment simply as the result of anger, and upon themselves merely as the victims of that anger ; and as a general rule punishment must be inflicted on children with great caution, that they may understand that its one aim is their improvement. It is foolish to cause children, when they are punished, to return thanks for the punishment by kissing hands,[1] and only turns the child into a slave. If physical punishment is often repeated, it makes a child stubborn ;

[1] This refers to the then very common German custom of making children who have been punished, actually express their gratitude by saying 'Danke schön,' and by kissing the hands of the person who has punished them.—(Tr.)

and if parents punish their children for obstinacy, they often become all the more obstinate. Besides, it is not always the worst men who are obstinate, and they will often yield easily to kind remonstrance.

86. The obedience of the growing *youth* must be distinguished from the obedience of the *child*. The former consists in submission to rules of duty. To do something for the sake of duty means obeying reason. It is in vain to speak to children of duty. They look upon it in the end as something which if not fulfilled will be followed by the rod. A child may be guided by mere instinct. As he grows up, however, the idea of duty must come in. Also the idea of shame should not be made use of with children, but only with those who have left childhood for youth. For it cannot exist with them till the idea of honour has first taken root.

87. The second principal feature in the formation of a child's character is *truthfulness*. This is the foundation and very essence of character. A man who tells lies has no character, and if he has any good in him it is merely the result of a certain kind of temperament. Some children have an inclination towards

lying, and this frequently for no other reason than that they have a lively imagination. It is the father's business to see that they are broken of this habit, for mothers generally look upon it as a matter of little or no importance, even finding in it a flattering proof of the cleverness and ability of their children. This is the time to make use of the sense of shame, for the child in this case will understand it well. The blush of shame betrays us when we lie, but it is not always a proof of it, for we often blush at the shamelessness of others who accuse us of guilt. On no condition must we punish children to force the truth from them, unless their telling a lie immediately results in some mischief; *then* they may be punished for that mischief. The withdrawal of respect is the only fit punishment for lying.

Punishments may be divided into *negative* and *positive* punishments. The first may be applied to laziness or viciousness; [1] for instance, lying, disobedience. Positive punishment may be applied to acts of spitefulness. But above all things we must take care never to bear children a grudge.

[1] Rink and Schubert add: 'quarrelsomeness.'—(Tr.)

88. A third feature in the child's character is *sociableness.* He must form friendships with other children, and not be always by himself. Some teachers, it is true, are opposed to these friendships in schools, but this is a great mistake. Children ought to prepare themselves for the sweetest enjoyment of life.

If a teacher allows himself to prefer one child to another, it must be on account of its character, and not for the sake of any talents the child may possess; otherwise jealousy will arise, which is opposed to friendship.

Children ought to be open-hearted and cheerful in their looks as the sun. A joyful heart alone is able to find its happiness in the good. A religion which makes people gloomy is a false religion; for we should serve God with a joyful heart, and not of constraint.

Children should sometimes be released from the narrow constraint of school, otherwise their natural joyousness will soon be quenched. When the child is set free he soon recovers his natural elasticity. Those games in which children, enjoying perfect freedom, are ever trying to outdo one another, will serve this purpose best, and they will soon make their minds bright and cheerful again.

89. Many people imagine that the years of their youth are the pleasantest and best of their lives; but it is not really so. They are the most troublesome; for we are then under strict discipline, can seldom choose our own friends, and still more seldom can we have our freedom. As Horace says: *Multa tulit, fecitque puer, sudavit et alsit.*[1]

90. Children should only be taught those things which are suited to their age. Many parents are pleased with the precocity of their offspring; but as a rule, nothing will come of such children. A child should be clever, but only as a child. He should not ape the manners of his elders. For a child to provide himself with moral sentences proper to manhood is to go quite beyond his province and to become merely an imitator. He ought to have merely the understanding of a child, and not seek to display it too early. A precocious child will never become a man of insight and clear understanding. It is just as much out of place for a

[1] The lad [who hopes to win the race] has borne and done much; he has endured extremes of heat and cold.

child to follow all the fashions of the time, to curl his hair, wear ruffles, and even carry a snuff-box. He will thus acquire affected manners not becoming to a child. Polite society is a burden to him, and he entirely lacks a man's heart. For that very reason we must set ourselves early to fight against all signs of vanity in a child; or, rather, we must give him no occasion to become vain. This easily happens by people prattling before children, telling them how beautiful they are, and how well this or that dress becomes them, and promising them some finery or other as a reward. Finery is not suitable for children. They must accept their neat and simple clothes as necessaries merely.

At the same time the parents must not set great store by their own clothes, nor admire themselves; for here, as everywhere, example is all-powerful, and either strengthens or destroys good precepts.

CHAPTER VI

91. PRACTICAL education includes (1) skill, (2) discretion, and (3) morality.

With regard to *skill*, we must see that it is thorough, and not superficial. We must not pretend to know things which we afterwards cannot accomplish. Skill must be characterised by thoroughness, and this thoroughness should gradually become a habit. Thoroughness is an essential element in the formation of a man's character, while skill is necessary for talent.

92. As regards *discretion*, it consists in the art of turning our skill to account; that is, of using our fellow-men for our own ends. For this several things are necessary. Properly speaking, it is the last quality attained by man, but it ranks second in importance.

In order that a child may acquire prudence, he must learn to disguise his feelings and to be reserved, while at the same time he learns to read the character of others. It is chiefly with regard to his own character that he must cultivate reserve. Decorum is the art of outward behaviour, and this is an art that we must possess. It is difficult to read the characters of others, but we must learn to do this without losing our own reserve. For this end a kind of dissembling is necessary; that is to say, we have to hide our faults and keep up that outward appearance. This is not necessarily deceit, and is sometimes allowable, *although* it does border closely on insincerity.

Dissimulation, however, is but a desperate expedient. To be prudent it is necessary that we should not lose our temper; on the other hand, we should not be too apathetic. A man should be brave without being violent—two qualities which are quite distinct. A brave man is one who is desirous of exercising his will. This desire necessitates control of the passions. Discretion is a matter of temperament.

93. *Morality* is a matter of character. *Sustine et abstine*,[1] such is the preparation for a wise moderation. The first step towards the

---

[1] Endure and abstain.

formation of a good character is to put our
passions on one side. We must take care that
our desires and inclinations do not become
passions, by learning to go without those things
that are denied to us. *Sustine* implies endure
and accustom thyself to endure. Courage and
a certain bent of mind towards it are necessary
for renunciation. We ought to accustom ourselves to opposition, the refusal of our requests,
and so on.

' Sympathy '[1] is a matter of temperament.
Children, however, ought to be prevented from
contracting the habit of a sentimental maudlin
sympathy. ' Sympathy ' is really sensitiveness,
and belongs only to characters of delicate feeling. It is distinct from compassion, and it is
an evil, consisting as it does merely in lament-

---

[1] Kant uses the word ' sympathy ' (*Sympathie*) not in the
usual sense which the word has in both German and English,
but in the more restricted sense of mere feeling for suffering,
which does not lead to helpful action, while compassion
(*Mitleid*) is fellow-feeling combined with a desire to help.
Sympathy is passive; compassion is active.

Cf. Kant's ' Tugendlehre ' (*Werke*, vol. ix. p. 317), where he
says that sympathy with joy or sorrow—' Mitfreude und Mit-
leiden (*sympathia moralis*) '—are mere feelings, and therefore
cannot be spoken of as moral duties, but that the duty consists in using these feelings as means for active and reasonable benevolence (' als Mittel zur Beförderung des thätigen
und vernünftigen Wohlwollens ').—(Tr.)

ing over a thing. It is a good thing to give children some pocket-money of their own, that they may help the needy; and in this way we should see if they are really compassionate or not. But if they are only charitable with their parents' money, we have no such test.

The saying *Festina lente* expresses constant activity, by which we must hasten to learn a great deal—that is, *festina.* But we must also learn thoroughly, and this needs time; that is, *lente.* The question here arises whether it is better to know a great many things in a superficial way or a few things thoroughly. It is better to know but little, and that little thoroughly, than to know a great deal and that superficially; for one becomes aware of the shallowness of superficial knowledge later on. But the child does not know as yet in what condition he may be with regard to requiring this or that branch of knowledge: it is best, therefore, that he should know something thoroughly of all, otherwise he will but deceive and dazzle others by his superficially acquired knowledge.

94. Our ultimate aim is the formation of *character*. Character consists in the firm pur-

pose to accomplish something, and then also in the actual accomplishing of it. *Vir propositi tenax*,[1] said Horace, and this is a good character. For instance, if a man makes a promise, he must keep it, however inconvenient it may be to himself; for a man who makes a resolution and fails to keep it will have no more confidence in himself. Suppose, for example, that a man resolves to rise early every morning that he may study, or do something or other, or take a walk—and excuses himself in spring because the mornings are still too cold, and rising early might injure his health, and in summer because it is well to allow himself to sleep, and sleep is pleasant—thus he puts off his resolution from day to day, until he ends in having no confidence in himself.

Those things which are contrary to morality must be excluded from such resolutions. The character of a wicked man is evil; but then, in this case, we do not call it 'character' any longer, but obstinacy; and yet there is still a certain satisfaction to find such a man holding fast to his resolutions and carrying them out,

---

[1] A man who keeps steadfast to his purpose.

though it would be much better if he showed the same persistency in good things.

Those who delay to fulfil their resolutions will do but little in life. We cannot expect much good to come of so-called future conversion. The sudden conversion of a man who has led a vicious life cannot possibly be enduring, in that it would be nothing short of a miracle to expect a man who has lived in such a way suddenly to assume the well-conducted life of a man who has always had good and upright thoughts. For the same reason we can expect no good to come from pilgrimages, mortifications, and fastings ; for it is difficult to see how such customs can, all at once, make a virtuous man out of a vicious one. How can it make a man more upright, or improve him in any way, to fast by day and to feast at night ; to impose a penance upon his body, which can in no way help towards improving his mind ?

95. *To form the foundation of moral character in children*, we must observe the following :—

We must place before them the duties they have to perform, as far as possible, by examples and rules. The duties which a child has to fulfil are only the common duties towards himself and towards others.   These duties must be the natural outcome of the kind of question involved.   We have thus to consider more closely :—

(1) *The child's duties towards himself.*—These do not consist in putting on fine clothes, in having sumptuous dinners, and so on, although his food should be good and his clothing neat. They do not consist in seeking to satisfy his cravings and inclinations ; for, on the contrary, he ought to be very temperate and abstemious. But they consist in his being conscious that man possesses a certain dignity, which ennobles him above all other creatures, and that it is his duty so to act as not to violate in his own person this dignity of mankind.   We are acting contrary to the dignity of man, for instance, when we give way to drink, or commit unnatural sins, or practise all kinds of irregularities, and so on, all of which place man far below the animals.   Further, to be cringing in one's behaviour to others ; to be always paying compliments, in order by such undignified conduct to ingratiate ourselves, as we assume—all this is against the dignity of man.

We can easily find opportunities for making children conscious of the dignity of man, even in their own persons. For instance, in the case of uncleanliness, which is at least unbecoming to mankind. But it is really through lying that a child degrades himself below the dignity of man, since lying presupposes the power of thinking and of communicating one's thoughts to others. Lying makes a man the object of common contempt, and is a means of robbing him of the respect for and trust in himself that every man should have.

(2) *The child's duties towards others.*—A child should learn early to reverence and respect the rights of others, and we must be careful to see that this reverence is realised in his actions. For instance, were a child to meet another poorer child and to push him rudely away, or to hit him, and so on, we must not say to the aggressor, 'Don't do that, you will hurt him; you should have pity, he is a poor child,' and so on. But we must treat him in the same haughty manner, because his conduct is against the rights of man. Children have as yet no idea, properly speaking, of generosity. We may, for instance, notice that when a child is told by his parents to share his slice of bread-and-butter with another, without being promised a second slice, the child either

refuses to obey, or obeys unwillingly. It is, besides, useless to talk to a child of generosity, as it is not yet in his power to be generous.

96. Many writers—Crugott, for instance— have either quite omitted, or explained falsely, that chapter of morality which teaches *our duties towards ourselves.* Our duties towards ourselves consist, as has been already said, in guarding, each in our own person, the dignity of mankind. A man will only reproach himself if he has the idea of mankind before his eyes. In this idea he finds an original, with which he compares himself. But when years increase, then is the critical period in which the idea of the dignity of man alone will suffice to keep the young man in bounds. But the youth must have some timely hints which will help him to know what he is to approve and what to mistrust.

97. Almost all our schools are lacking in something which would nevertheless greatly tend to the formation of uprightness in children— namely, a *catechism of right conduct.* This should contain, in a popular form, everyday questions of right and wrong. For instance, a man has a certain debt to pay to-day, but he sees another man in sore need, and, moved with pity, gives him the money which belongs of right to his creditor. Is this right or wrong?

It is wrong, for we must be free from obligation before we can be generous. When we give alms, we do a meritorious act; but in paying our debts, we do what we are bound to do.

Again, can a lie ever be justified by necessity? No, there is no single instance in which a lie can be justified. If this rule were not strictly adhered to, children especially would take the smallest excuse for a necessity, and would very often allow themselves to tell lies. If there were a book of this kind, an hour might very profitably be spent daily in studying it, so that children might learn and take to heart lessons on right conduct—that apple of God's eye upon earth.

98. As to the *obligation of benevolence*, it is not an absolute obligation. We must arouse the sympathies of children, not so much to feel for the sorrows of others as to a sense of their duty to help them. Children ought not to be full of feeling, but they should be full of the idea of duty. Many people, indeed, become hardhearted, where once they were pitiful, because they have so often been deceived. It is in vain to point out to children the meritorious side of actions. Religious teachers often make the mistake of representing acts of benevolence as meritorious, without seeing that all we can do for God is just to do what we are bound to do; and in doing good to the poor, we are only doing our duty. For the inequality of man arises only from accidental circumstances—if I possess wealth, to what do I owe it but to the laying hold of circumstances favourable to me or to my predecessors?—while our consideration of the whole remains ever the same.

99. We only excite envy in a child by telling him to compare his own worth with the worth of others. He ought rather to compare himself with a concept of his reason. For humility is really nothing else than the comparing of our own worth with the standard of moral perfection. Thus, for instance, the Christian religion makes people humble, not by preaching humility, but by teaching them to compare themselves with the highest pattern of perfection. It is very absurd to see humility in depreciating ourselves. 'See how such and such a child behaves himself!' An exclamation of this kind produces only a very ignoble mode of thinking;

for if a man estimates his own worth by the worth of others, he either tries to elevate himself above others or to detract from another's worth. But this last is envy. We then only seek to impute faults to others, in order that we may compare favourably with them. Thus the spirit of emulation, wrongly applied, only arouses envy. Emulation may occasionally be used to good purpose, as when we tell a child, in order to convince him of the possibility of performing a certain task, that others could easily do it. We must on no account allow one child to humiliate another. We must seek to avoid every form of pride which is founded upon superiority of fortune. At the same time we must seek to cultivate frankness in the child. This is an unassuming confidence in himself, the possession of which places him in a position to exhibit his talents in a becoming manner. This self-confidence is to be distinguished from insolence, which is really indifference to the judgment of others.

100. All the cravings of men are either formal (relating to freedom and power), or material (set upon a certain object)—that is to say, either cravings of imagination or enjoyment—or,

finally, cravings for the continuation of these two things as elements of happiness.   Cravings of the first kind are the lust of honour (ambition), the lust of power, and the lust of possession. Those of the second kind are sexual indulgence (voluptuousness), enjoyment of good things (good living), or the enjoyment of social intercourse (love of amusement).

Cravings of the third kind, finally, are love of life, love of health, and love of ease (freedom from care as regards the future).

Vices are either those of malice, baseness, or narrow-mindedness.

To the first belong envy, ingratitude, and joy at the misfortune of others. To the second kind belong injustice, unfaithfulness (deceitfulness), dissoluteness—and this in the squandering of wealth as well as of health (intemperance) and of honour.

Vices of the third kind are those of unkindness, niggardliness, and idleness (effeminacy).

101. *Virtues* are either virtues of merit or merely of obligation or of innocence.

To the first belong magnanimity (shown in self-conquest in times of anger or when tempted to ease and the lust of possession), benevolence, and self-command.

To the second belong honesty, propriety, peaceableness ; and to the third, finally, belong honourableness, modesty, and content.

102. But is man by nature morally good or bad ? He is neither, for he is not by nature a moral being. He only becomes a moral being when his reason has developed ideas of duty and law. One may say, however, that he has a natural inclination to every vice, for he has inclinations and instincts which would urge him one way, while his reason would drive him in another. He can only become morally good by means of virtue—that is to say, by self-restraint— though he may be innocent as long as his vicious inclinations lie dormant.

Vices, for the most part, arise in this way, that civilisation does violence to Nature ; and yet our destiny as human beings is to emerge from our natural state as animals. Perfect art becomes second nature.

103. Everything in education depends upon establishing correct principles, and leading children to understand and accept them. They must learn to substitute abhorrence for what is

revolting and absurd, for hatred; the fear of
their own conscience, for the fear of man and
divine punishment; self-respect and inward
dignity, for the opinions of men; the inner value
of actions, for words and mere impulses; understanding, for feeling; and joyousness and piety
with good humour, for a morose, timid, and
gloomy devotion.

But above all things we must keep children
from esteeming the *merita fortunæ* [1] too highly.

104. In looking at the education of children
with regard to *religion*, the first question which
arises is whether it is practicable to impart
religious ideas to children early in life.   On this
point much has been written in educational
works. Religious ideas always imply a theology;
and how can young people be taught theology
when they do not yet know themselves, much
less the world?   Is the youth who as yet
knows nothing of duty in the condition to
comprehend an immediate duty towards God?
This much is certain—that, could it be brought
about that children should never witness a single
act of veneration to God, never even hear the
name of God spoken, it might then be the right

[1] Strokes of luck.

order of things to teach them first about ends
and aims, and of what concerns mankind; to
sharpen their judgment; to instruct them in the
order and beauty of the works of Nature; then
add a wider knowledge of the structure of the
universe; and then only might be revealed to
them for the first time the idea of a Supreme
Being—a Law-giver. But since this mode of
proceeding is impossible, according to the
present condition of society, and we cannot
prevent children from hearing the name of God
and seeing tokens of man's devotion to Him; if
we were to teach them something about God
only when they are grown up, the result would
be either indifference or false ideas—for instance,
terror of God's power. Since, then, it is to be
feared that such ideas might find a dwelling-
place in the child's imagination, to avoid it we
should seek early to impart religious ideas to
the child. But this instruction must not be
merely the work of memory and imitation; the
way chosen must be always in accordance with
Nature. Children will understand—without
abstract ideas of duty, of obligations, of good
and bad conduct—that there is a law of duty
which is not the same as ease, utility, or other

considerations of the kind, but something universal, which is not governed by the caprice of men. The teacher himself, however, must form this idea.

At first we must ascribe everything to Nature, and afterwards Nature herself to God; showing at first, for instance, how everything is disposed for the preservation of the species and their equilibrium, but at the same time with consideration in the long run for man, that he may attain happiness.

The idea of God might first be taught by analogy with that of a father under whose care we are placed, and in this way we may with advantage point out to the child the unity of men as represented by one family.

105. What, then, is *religion*? Religion is the law in us, in so far as it derives emphasis from a Law-giver and a Judge above us. It is morality applied to the knowledge of God. If religion is not united to morality, it becomes merely an endeavour to win favour. Hymn-singing, prayers, and church-going should only give men fresh strength, fresh courage to advance; or they should be the utterance of a heart inspired with the idea of duty. They

are but preparations for good works, and not
the works themselves; and the only real way
in which we may please God is by our becoming better men.

In teaching a child we must first begin with
the law which is in him. A vicious man is
contemptible to himself, and this contempt is
inborn, and does not arise in the first instance
because God has forbidden vice; for it does
not necessarily follow that the law-giver is the
author of the law. A prince, for instance, may
forbid stealing in his country without being
called the original prohibitor of theft. From
this, man learns to understand that it is a good
life alone which makes him worthy of happiness.
The divine law must at the same time be recog-
nised as Nature's law, for it is not arbitrary.
Hence religion belongs to all morality.

We must not, however, begin with theology.
The religion which is founded merely on
theology can never contain anything of morality.
Hence we derive no other feelings from it but
fear on the one hand, and hope of reward on
the other, and this produces merely a super-
stitious cult. Morality, then, must come first
and theology follow; and that is religion.

106. The law that is within us we call conscience. Conscience, properly speaking, is the application of our actions to this law. The reproaches of conscience would be without effect, if we did not regard it as the representative of God, who, while He has raised up a tribunal over us, has also established a judgment-seat within us. If religion is not added to moral conscientiousness, it is of no effect. Religion without moral conscientiousness is a service of superstition. People will serve God by praising Him and reverencing His power and wisdom, without thinking how to fulfil the divine law; nay, even without knowing and searching out His power, wisdom, and so on. These hymn-singings are an opiate for the conscience of such people, and a pillow upon which it may quietly slumber.

107. Children cannot comprehend all *religious ideas*, notwithstanding there are some which we ought to teach them; these, however, must be more negative than positive. It is of no use whatever to let children recite formulæ; it only produces a misconception of piety. The true way of honouring God consists in acting in accordance with His will, and this is

what we must teach children to do. We must
see to it that the name of God is not so often
taken in vain, and this by ourselves as well as
by children. If we use it in congratulating our
friends—even with pious intent—this also is
a misuse of the holy name. The idea of God
ought to fill people with reverence every time
they hear His name spoken. And it should be
pronounced but seldom and never lightly. The
child must learn to feel reverence towards
God, as the Lord of life and of the whole
world; further, as one who cares for men, and
lastly as their Judge. We are told of Newton
that he never pronounced the name of God
without pausing for a while and meditating
upon it.

108. Through an explanation which unites
the ideas of *God* and of *duty* the child learns
the better to respect the divine care for creatures,
and will thus be kept from an inclination towards
destruction and cruelty, which we so often see
in the torture of small animals. At the same
time we should teach the child to discover good
in evil. For instance, beasts of prey and insects
are patterns of cleanliness and diligence; so,
too, evil men are a warning to follow the law;

and birds, by waylaying worms, protect the garden ; and so on.

109. We must, then, give children some idea of the Supreme Being, in order that when they see others praying, and so on, they may know to whom they are praying, and why. But these ideas must be few in number, and, as has been said, merely negative. We must begin to impart them from early youth, being careful at the same time that they do not esteem men according to their religious observances, for, in spite of the diversity of religions, religion is everywhere the same.

110. Here, in conclusion, we shall add a few remarks which should especially be observed by the youth as he approaches the *years of early manhood.* At this time the youth begins to make certain distinctions which he did not make formerly. In the first place, the distinction of *sex.* Nature has spread a certain veil of secrecy over this subject, as if it were something unseemly for man, and merely an animal need in him. She has, however, sought to unite it, as far as possible, with every kind of morality. Even savage nations behave with a kind of shame and reserve in this matter. Children

now and then ask curious questions ; for instance,
' Where do children come from ? ' &c. They are,
however, easily satisfied either at receiving an
unreasonable answer which means nothing, or
by being told that these are childish questions.

These inclinations develop mechanically in
the youth, and, as is the way with all instincts,
even without the knowledge of a particular
object. Thus it is impossible to keep the youth in
ignorance and the innocence which belongs to
ignorance. By silence the evil is but increased.
We see this in the education of our forefathers.
In the education of the present day it is rightly
assumed that we must speak openly, clearly, and
definitely with the youth. We must allow that
it is a delicate point, for we cannot look upon it
as a subject for open conversation ; but if we
enter with sympathy into his new impulses [1] all
will go well.

The thirteenth or fourteenth year is usually
the time in which the feeling of sex develops
itself in the youth. (When it happens earlier it
is because children have been led astray and
corrupted through bad examples.) Their judg-

[1] Rink and Schubert add : ' and discuss it with him in all
earnestness.'—(Tr.)

ment also is then already formed, and at about this time Nature has prepared them for our discussing this matter with them.

111. Nothing weakens the mind as well as the body so much as the kind of lust which is directed towards themselves, and it is entirely at variance with the nature of man. But this also must not be concealed from the youth. We must place it before him in all its horribleness, telling him that in this way he will become useless for the propagation of the race, that his bodily strength will be ruined by this vice more than by anything else, that he will bring on himself premature old age, and that his intellect will be very much weakened, and so on.

We may escape from these impulses by constant occupation, and by devoting no more time to bed and sleep than is necessary. Through this constant occupation we may banish all such thoughts from our mind, for even if the object only remains in our imagination it eats away our vital strength. If we direct our inclination towards the other sex, there are at any rate certain obstacles in the way; if, however, they are directed towards ourselves, we may satisfy them at any time. The physical effects

are extremely hurtful, but the consequences
with regard to morality are even worse. The
bounds of Nature are here overstepped and the
inclination rages ceaselessly, since no real satisfaction can take place. The teachers of grown-
up youths have propounded the question whether
it is allowable for a youth to enter into relations
with the other sex? If we must choose one of
the two things, this is certainly better than the
other. In the former he acts against Nature;
in the latter he does not. Nature has called
upon him to be a man so soon as he becomes of
age, and to propagate his kind; the exigences,
however, which exist for man in a civilised
community render it sometimes impossible for
him to marry and educate his children at that
period. Herein he would be transgressing the
social order. It is the best way—indeed, it is
the duty of the young man—to wait till he is in
a condition to marry. He acts then not only
as a good man, but as a good citizen.

The youth should learn early to entertain a
proper respect for the other sex; to win their
esteem by an activity free from vice; and thus
to strive after the high prize of a happy
marriage.

112. A second distinction which the youth begins to make about the time of his entrance into society consists in the knowledge of the *distinction of rank* and the *inequality of men.* As a child he must not be allowed to notice this. He must not even be allowed to give orders to the servants. If the child sees his parents giving orders to the servants, they may at any rate say to him : 'We give them their bread, and therefore they obey us—you do not, and therefore they need not obey you.' In fact, children would of themselves know nothing of this distinction, if only their parents did not give them this false notion. The young man should be shown that the inequality of man is an institution that has arisen on account of one man striving to get an advantage over another. The consciousness of the equality of men, together with their civil inequality, may be taught him little by little.

113. We must accustom the youth to esteem himself absolutely and not relatively to others. The high esteem of others for what does not constitute the true value of men at all is vanity. Further, we must teach him to be conscientious in everything, and not merely to appear so, but to strive to be so. We must also make him heedful that in no matter about which he has well weighed a resolution shall it remain an empty resolution. Rather than this it is better to conceive of no resolution at all, and let the matter remain in doubt. He must be taught contentedness as regards outward circumstances, and patience in work— *Sustine et abstine*—moderation in pleasure. If we are not always thinking of pleasure, but will be patient in our work, we shall become useful members of the community and be kept from *ennui*.

Again, we must encourage the youth—

(1) To be cheerful and good-humoured. Cheerfulness arises from the fact of having nothing to reproach oneself with.

(2) To be even-tempered. By means of self-discipline one can train oneself to become a cheerful companion in society.

(3) To regard many things invariably as matters of duty. We must hold an action to be worthy, not because it falls in with our inclinations, but because in performing it we fulfil our duty.

(4) In love towards others, as well as to

feelings of cosmopolitanism. There exists something in our minds which causes us to take an interest (*a*) in ourselves, (*b*) in those with whom we have been brought up, and (*c*) there should also be an interest in the progress of the world. Children should be made acquainted with this interest, so that it may give warmth to their hearts. They should learn to rejoice at the world's progress, although it may not be to their own advantage or to that of their country.

(5) To set little store by the enjoyment of the good things of life. The childish fear of death will then disappear—we must point out to the youth that the anticipations of pleasure are not realised in its fulfilment.

Lastly, by pointing out the necessity of daily ' settling accounts ' with himself, so that at the end of life he may be able to make an estimate with regard to its value.

SELECTED ANN ARBOR PAPERBACKS

works of enduring merit